highway of
sleeping towns

haiku and senryu

DEBORAH P KOLODJI

highway of sleeping towns

Hubble-Magellan Composite of M83 courtesy of NASA and the Hubble Space Telescope Team

Author photo on back cover by Naia

Library of Congress Control Number: 2016943998

ISBN: 978-0-9915772-3-1

Published by Shabda Press
Pasadena, CA 91107
www.shabdapress.com

In memory of my parents:

John H. Anderson, Jr., who always loved a good road trip
Aileen Anderson, who found joy in dogs, horses, and hardwood forests

white marble
I am small at the feet
of Lincoln

summer moonrise
the distance between sea stars
shrinking

the ocean
spills its secrets—
two sandpipers

a bull frog
hits the lower register
weeping willow song

floating purple—
my daydreams follow
the water hyacinth

molten sunset
a black-bellied plover
on the inlet beach

train station—
the flutter of wings
in a chandelier

loading his bicycle
on the bus
a dozen roses

highway
of sleeping towns
the milky way

a dog barks
after moonset
perseids

lengthening nights
a village
made of Lincoln logs

gull cry
a morning's layers
of gray

salt wind
each step in the sand
a bit deeper

gentle sway of kelp
along wooden docks
summer sea

the creek
where she was baptized
sun after rain

her bare feet
on the path ahead
hummingbird sage

thistles in bloom
grandmother's needle
threaded with purple

the quilt she made me
forty years ago
winter rain

his oxygen tube
stretches the length of the house
winter seclusion

live jazz
the sea bass
in reduction sauce

sun ray
through stained glass
his favorite hymn

seagull moon
the sky still blue
this evening

police helicopter
over the estuary
terns

neither of us budges
the heavy anchor chains
of a tanker ship

summer chill
a man guts sculpin
at the fish mart

we promise each other
nothing will change
slack tide

last persimmon
the real estate agent
suggests a lower price

rust in the cedars
the quiet interrupted
by heron-cry

talk radio
a swirl of gnats
in my headlights

white smoke
we remember why we don't
talk of religion

to disturb
the sleep of gulls
the milky way

cancelled flight
the landing
of cormorants

cold summer
one suitcase circling
baggage claim

the pond
where koi once swam
shadows of willows

moon bridge
a woman broken
by spring ripples

our moment gone now
dry iris by the stone lantern

only my eyes
and the ox-eye daisies
dune silence

old arguments
the purple-edged leaves
of Thai basil

fountain
on her cheeks
pennies

boundary waters
the cry of a loon
by my canoe

cucumber salad
the cold look
after a breakup

one mistake
after another . . .
falling leaves

moving day
the clatter of marbles
in a shoe box

in spite of your silence the birth of stars

dried corsage
almost dust now . . .
the way we were

settling the estate
empty gum wrappers
in her purse

deep winter
the faded coffee mug
that says "grandpa"

the scarf
she never finished
brown pine needles

matillija poppies
the appliance repairman
comes the wrong day

half-blown dandelion
my neighbor's daughter
moves back in

nimbostratus
the gray of his army
underwear

new year's rain
the quietness
of living alone

trillium
under the redwoods
her lace camisole

what happens
in Seattle stays in Seattle
rain

late jacaranda
the bridesmaid dress
too small

the green
beneath her kayak
eelgrass

unopened rosebud
on a broken stem
miscarriage

the wait
to take a driving test . . .
ants on the sidewalk

gray morning
the whole world
a fog horn

sometimes
there's nothing left
dried apricots

her old cd
on the long drive
wild mustard

waking up
to the scent of redwoods
distant birdsong

Bollywood
shadows in the folds
of our napkins

lock of hair
in the top dresser drawer. . .
that O. Henry story

the TSA agent
inspects my medication
spring melancholy

bats on top
of the deodars
waning moon

roadside wildflowers
a cop's bright lights
in my rearview mirror

morning physics
a paper airplane glides
out the window

I didn't know
the dark side of the moon
the dark side of you

night-blooming jasmine
uncomfortable memories
of us

garden whispers
the air heavy
with magnolia

tax day
my mother's IV
beeps at me

love letter
the meadow unkempt
with tidy-tips

still asleep
with the sun half up
1000 thread count

the square root
of negative one
clouds

as far
as the moon's dark side
his untouched pillow

moon rock
behind the glass
summer divorce

lingering buckwheat morning wren

honey mesquite
the worried chip chip chip
of a Gambel's quail

Euler's number
your litany
of unrepeatable excuses

Monday rain
a line of ants edges
the shower door

chopped onions
on a new cutting board
divorce papers

all the birds
in my neighbor's tree
custody agreement

lingerie drawer
after the divorce
skimpier

sidewalk ATM
a deposit slip picked up
by the spring breeze

liquor store
his ID
of a dark-eyed junco

potted narcissus
in a California window
White Christmas

moss spreads
on the walkway
our silence

too many sneakers
the Chinese elm
still dropping leaves

first light
through the kitchen window
our milk mustaches

the undiscovered country
a cereal box full
of cupboard moths

pi day
the circumference
of an onion slice

donkey tail plant
an argument
with tech support

cinnamon hand lotion
the pie charts
in her PowerPoint

smoke bush
even my dreams
muted mauve

request
for a parent-teacher conference
wild mushroom soup

a crackle of fireworks the echo of dogs

potted poinsettias
at the holiday party
bullets

off-topic
a turkey vulture's
increasing loops

aftershocks
the tremble in his voice
when he calls me

dead wood
woven in with the living
juniper bonsai

Liszt birthday concert
I shrink inside
the Spreckels Organ

dimes and quarters
fall out of his pocket
perseids

the call
we've been dreading
lemon blossoms

counting raindrops
binomial coefficients
of my roof

moonless night
above our campfire
the milky way

lake clouds
the gurgle
of unmentionable things

the world so big
without you in it
summer sea

inbound ferry
the bobbing head
of a harbor seal

morning tidepools
a hermit crab tries on
the bottle cap

my steps
your steps
morning sand

pulsing sea jellies
a symphony orchestra
on mute

drones the year of the horse nebula

murder of crows
I write his name
on a sugar skull

concertina echoes . . .
the gnarled trunk
of an olive tree

toccata in c
rainy afternoon
in Balboa Park

fallen rose petals
on Colorado Boulevard
our New Year's smiles

calendar filled
with doctor's appointments
fallen jacaranda

mockingbird
in the purple leaf plum
morning stillness

walnut pie
the family reunion
without her

echoes of polkas
a row of empty
accordion cases

rows of holes
in the woodpecker tree
her passing

Fermat's Last Theorem
a jar of buttons
in a hoarder's garage

new moon weekend
a campground full
of telescopes

first daffodils
she finally restrings
his old guitar

a plane takes off
into the cloudless sky
custody agreement

orionids—
even the sky can't sleep
tonight

a long discussion
about chemotherapy
winter fly

Gone with the Wind
an empty pillow
by the window seat

winter solitude
the company
of unshelved books

unopened magnolia
a small girl hops
from stone to stone

sum of the first n
odd numbers
duck pond

our history
written in rock
desert lavender

the rice
in our suitcase
honeymoon

virtual garden
she plants four seasons
of daffodils

his shoulders
in black leather
motorcycle wind

LA traffic
our lady of the perpetually
late

re-entry heat
he spends the night
on the couch

string theory—
a newspaper recycler's
collection bin

the sun's afterglow
a pile of shrimp shared
off a paper napkin

jade plant
tiny clusters of white
lies

brittlebush
not yet blooming
our vows

family tree
we compare
mosquito bites

windstorm
olive branches from a neighbor
I've never met

amidst all this grief…
plum blossoms
on my windshield

visiting hours
at the nursing station
tissue paper roses

remnants of rain
between the flagstones
morning prayer

Gregorian chant . . .
reaching for
my quiet place

shorter days
the pastor's sermon
longer

the wait
for her death certificate
hazy sky

a caterpillar's progress
across the fallen leaf
jet lag

desert heat
one mesquite seed
suspended mid-air

uncarved pumpkins
the pregnant woman
strokes her belly

midsummer quiet
the cascading shades
of mountain ridges

a bird's broken wing
my grandfather fails
the driving test

centering my thoughts leaf labyrinth

tidal drift
one harbor seal
noses another

deep space
a friendship dissolving
in close quarters

cosine of an angle
he changes political
parties

asparagus
a delicate alignment
of interests

low tide
under Cassiopeia
loneliness

Christmas light test
trying to untangle
last year

morning glory vines
a coil of barbed wire
on the fence top

dozen red roses
she examines the bruise
in the mirror

Hiroshima Day
in the friendship garden
flashes of koi

blueberry green tea
my five minute break
becomes ten

sharp words
her holiday collection
of cookie cutters

the meme
from your photo
blowfish

leonids—
the sparkle
in her laugh

home again
after a week on the road
plum blossoms

language app
we compare passport
photos

six ants
come out of his laptop
summer school

Moonlight Sonata
the dance
of a crane fly

yellow pine forest
the different purples
of lupine

summer quiet
the stars dare me
to count them

big sky country
my horse races
the milky way

roadside bison
the cowboy aims
his digital camera

close approach
I meet an old friend
to see Mars

light speed
a century ahead
of his speeding ticket

Texas moon
the smell of refinery lights
by the highway

waning sun
along the coast
poison hemlock

the beach
emptier and emptier
moonless night

another blue sky
another day without you
apple blossom rain

again
that funeral parlor smell
Easter lily

a towhee's voice
somewhere
mountain lilac

slow day
even the planes
in a holding pattern

spring shadows
the hollow sound
of bamboo

topology
of a donut hole
winter rain

cottonwood rattle
the wordlessness
of his final days

fallen rose petals
my mother's dog
misses her too

rusty lichen
on the granite rock
old promises

desert moon
the twisted shadow
of a Joshua tree

slow moving clock
the Norman Rockwell print
in the waiting room

crisp bites
of a gala apple
office gossip

lulled by the sound
of a horse eating hay
early summer

two crows
in the apple orchard
thunder

tree snag—
not that much left
of us

Avogadro constant
fifty pounds later
still a "B" cup

warmed up
by the crowd around me
a row of tuba players

sting ray
a flutter of life
in her belly

a flower blooms
where it shouldn't
premature baby

a river of corn lilies
divides the meadow
yellow butterfly

lock of baby hair
from his first haircut
my dreams for him

spent lilacs
the time warp
in her garden

pear blossoms
another parking ticket
for my stolen car

tarp-covered yacht
the longer shadows
of a fake owl

morning fog
my connecting flight
delayed again

Mt. Vesuvius
    the broken gear
on the time machine

short circuit
she activates
the flirting module

moonflower
a love letter
to Captain Kirk

x-ray eyes
can he see my heart
beating faster?

rainy season
I find out
he's married

tracing my name
in marble . . .
autumn loneliness

space walk
the blues
of our planet

fire sky
her library book
about dragons

the itch
in your absence
poison oak

that song
about dying young
spring rain

tea leaves
from Mt. Olympus
his sage advice

alone
after returning the ring
cherry blossom rain

salt breeze
over the pickleweed
marbled godwits

feeling romantic
she blows them a kiss
they remain frogs

sunset creeps
across the vineyard
afternoon chill

winter sea
the rise and fall
and fall

what's left of us
caves
on Mars

a lily floats
in a bowl of water
bank balance

blue damselfly
on a blade of grass
the quiet before leaving

whispers
in the waiting room
mother's MRI

taps . . .
all we could say
now said

silent cannon
at Gettysburg
birdsong

Acknowledgments

This collection spans fifteen years of my life as a haiku poet. I am immensely grateful to Jerry Ball, who founded the Southern California Haiku Study Group, becoming my first guide on the haiku path. Haiku can be a shared community experience, and I feel lucky to have attended years of Yuki Teikei Haiku Society retreats at Asilomar, as well as a number of Seabeck Haiku Getaways on the Hood Canal with Haiku Northwest. Members of the Southern California Haiku Study Group have simply become family.

Many of the poems in this collection were written during haiku walks (or ginko), and I want to thank my companions on the journey to explore the wild side of LA – Wendy Wright, Naia, Genie Nakano, Peggy Castro, Billie Dee, Victor Ortiz, Greg Longenecker, Bill Hart, Susan Rogers, Samantha Henderson (who once prevented me from accidently stepping off a cliff while photographing a wildflower), Ruth Nolan, Kathabela Wilson, Mary Torregrossa, Marcy Clements, James Won, Wakako Rollinger, and Peggy Hehman-Smith. Thanks to Denise Dumars, Kendall Evans, Sheila Finch, Dan Houston, Grant Farley, Marcia Behar, Jie Tian, Elva Lauter, Kim Esser, Phyllis Collins, Lynn Allgood, W. Gregory Stewart, Janis Lukstein, Lois P. Jones, Alice Pero, and many other writer/poet friends who have supported my writing. I am thankful for Patricia Machmiller and her calm supportive presence, Fay Aoyagi whose commentary on my haiku submissions are always helpful, and Michael Dylan Welch whose long discussions on anything related to haiku are always stimulating. Thanks to my family, especially my sister, Desiree McMahon, and, of course, my children, Kirk, Sean, and Yvette who always have my back.

With gratitude to the editors who first published many of the haiku and senryu in this collection in the following publications: *7x20, Acorn, Akitsu Quarterly, Altadena Poetry Review, The Aurorean, Bones, bottle rockets, Brass Bell, Chrysanthemum, coloradoboulevard.net, Daily Haiku, frogpond, Frozen Butterfly, Daily Yomiuri, Geppo, Grievous Angel, Haigaonline, Haiku Canada Review, Haiku Harvest, Haiku Headlines, Haiku Sun, Haikuniverse, Hermitage, The Heron's Nest, A Hundred Gourds, kernels, SARM (Romanian Society for Meteors and Astronomy), Lone Star Stories, Magazine of Speculative Poetry, The Mainichi, Mariposa, Mayfly, Modern Haiku, moongarlic, Moonset, Notes from the Gean, Phantom Seed, Poetry Life and Times, Prune Juice, Rattle, Riverbed Haiku, Roadrunner Haiku, Rumrazor Press, San Gabriel Valley Poetry Quarterly, The Shantytown Anomaly, Short Stuff, Simply Haiku, Sketchbook, Sonic Boom, South by Southeast, tinywords, Under the Basho, White Lotus, Wisteria,* and *World Haiku Review.*

A few haiku in this book appeared online in the Shiki Monthly Kukai, while others were featured in *Ants on the Sidewalk, Episode 26* of the *Haiku Chronicles*, a video montage podcast produced by Alan Pizzarelli and Donna Beaver. Poems in this volume also appeared in the Haiku Registry and Per Diem at the Haiku Foundation, *Silver Blade*, and Wednesday Haiku @Issa's Untidy Hut.

Some of these poems have been anthologized (a number as first publications) in *Aftershocks: The Poetry of Recovery* (Santa Lucia Books 2008), *Among the Lilies* (Shadows Ink, 2008), *Basho Challenge Chapbook* (Lilliput Review, 2010), *Caught in the Breeze* (Haiku Pacific Rim Anthology 2012), *Echoes* (Red Moon Press, 2007), *Faces and Places* (Living Haiku Anthology E-Book, 2014), *Haiku 21* (Modern Haiku Press, 2011), *Haiku North America Anthologies, Haiku Society of America Membership Anthologies, Halloween Haiku* (Popcorn Press, 2011), *Lighting a Candle* (Two Autumns Press, 2010), *Living Haiku Anthology* (online), *Nest Feathers: Selected Haiku from the First 15 Years of the Heron's Nest* (2015), *A New Resonance 4: Emerging Voices in English-Language Haiku* (Red Moon Press 2005) , *One Song* (Two Autumns Press, 2014), *Red Moon Anthologies, Rhysling Anthology* (Science Fiction Poetry Association, 2016), *The Sacred in Contemporary Haiku* (Robert Epstein, 2014), *San Diego Poetry Anthology* (2015), *Seabeck Haiku Getaway Anthologies, small canyons anthology* (HSA Southwest Region, 2010), *Southern California Haiku Study Group Anthologies, Red Door Anthology* (Caltech 2012), *The Temple Bell Stops: Contemporary Poems of Grief, Loss, and Change* (Modern English Tanka Press 2012), *World Haiku Anthology* (World Haiku Association 2008*)*, and *Yuki Teikei Haiku Society Membership Anthologies.*

To conclude, I'd like to thank Tim Green, the editor of *Rattle*, for first publishing the title haiku in the Japanese Forms Tribute, and Bill Hart for suggesting that it would make a good title poem. Thanks also to Naia, Sean Carlton, and Greg Longenecker for being early readers of the manuscript, Roberta Beary, Stanford Forrester, Terry Ann Carter, and Lois P. Jones for being willing to blurb the book, Naia for taking my photo on the cover, and Kirk, Sean, Yvette, and Werner for helping with proof-reading, and/or the giant living room project of sorting haiku on index cards. With much gratitude to the Southern California Haiku Study Group and the global haiku community, the Pasadena-area Poetry Community, and the members of my fiction writing groups who have supported and encouraged me throughout the years. Finally, thanks to Teresa Mei Chuc and Shabda Press for bringing a dream to fruition.

CPSIA information can be obtained
at www.ICGtesting.com
Printed in the USA
FSOW01n1011190417
33193FS